HAUS CURIOSITIES

*Self and Society*

# About the Contributors

**Michael Amherst** is the author of *Go the Way Your Blood Beats*, for which he received an award from Arts Council England and won the 2019 Stonewall Book Awards Israel Fishman Non-Fiction Award. His fiction has been longlisted for the BBC's Opening Lines showcase and the Bath Short Story Award, shortlisted for the Bridport Prize, and published in *The White Review*. He is a member of Writing West Midlands' Room 204 scheme.

**Tara McEvoy** is a press officer with Pushkin Press in London. She recently graduated with a PhD in English literature from Queen's University Belfast and edits Belfast-based magazine *The Tangerine*. Her work has been published in the *TLS*, *Vogue*, *The Observer*, *The Guardian*, *The Irish Times*, and *The Stinging Fly*.

**David Crane** is an international development consultant, having recently graduated with an MSc in development studies. He writes articles and essays on a variety of topics, primarily African economic and political history, conflict and stability, and forced migration.

**Nick Inman** is an author, translator, and journalist who writes mainly about Spain and France (where he lives). In a former life, he was an editor for DK Eyewitness Travel Guides. His books include *Politipedia* and, most recently, *A Guide to Mystical France*.

**Beninio McDonough-Tranza** recently completed an MA in global history. His research focuses on the intellectual history of European imperialism, and his first academic article is forthcoming in *Victorian Review*. His writing has appeared in *New Statesman*, *Hektoen International*, *The New Federalist*, and *Earth Island Journal*.

# SELF AND SOCIETY

Michael Amherst, Tara McEvoy, David Crane,
Nick Inman, and Beninio McDonough-Tranza

Foreword by Michael D. Higgins

First published by Haus Publishing in 2021
4 Cinnamon Row
London SW11 3TW
*www.hauspublishing.com*

'Autumn Journal' by Louis MacNeice
(Faber & Faber) reproduced by permission by
David Higham Associates

A CIP catalogue record for this book is
available from the British Library

Print ISBN: 978-1-913368-32-6
Ebook ISBN: 978-1-913368-33-3

Typeset in Garamond by MacGuru Ltd

Printed in the Czech Republic

# Contents

# Foreword

*President Michael D. Higgins*

I am delighted to congratulate all those who have submitted work for this year's Hubert Butler Essay Prize, taking the time to share with us their thoughts and insights on the relationship between communal solidarity and individual freedom. The themes and topics covered by the essays submitted are diverse and broad-ranging, but all are rooted in an interrogation of the values by which we must live together if we are to create a truly ethical world.

Today, appeals to the common good have taken on a new urgency; this is a time when we are asked to exercise our responsibilities to the best of our capacity from an ethic of Good Citizenship. Responding to the coronavirus crisis provides an opportunity for the world to do things better in the future, to accept shared responsibility for matters such as global poverty and climate change, to recover the sense of the collective that may have been numbed by a credo of individualism and uncritical, even insatiable, consumerism.

Hubert Butler, after whom this prize is named, was a man who marched, in the words of Roy Foster, with 'history looking over his shoulder', contesting, questioning, and never afraid to transcend the self in his pursuit of human rights and a more tolerant Europe. His courageous foresight and refusal to become circumscribed by limitations of self-interest enabled him to offer a greatly generous and humanistic vision towards the creation of a better world.

The American writer John Casey has written of how Hubert Butler, when writing about the children of Drancy or the friends he made in Russia between the wars, refuses to 'let them be reduced to statistical miniatures or to let them be swept up into the blurred majesty of epic'. Indeed, Butler himself in *The Children of Drancy* talks poignantly of how, by reducing the children of the Holocaust to cold statistics rather than small people reading stories and playing with toys, we dehumanise them, because 'their suffering is too great and protracted to be imagined, and the range of human sympathy is narrowly restricted'.

He is speaking, of course, about the intimacies of humanity and the great importance of scaling down the immense and the titanic to the shared vulnerability common to all humanity.

A deep awareness of that shared vulnerability is

present in so many of the essays submitted, as they examine and discuss some of the drivers of a trend towards individual rather than collective welfare, and call in their different ways for the articulation of new models of coexistence. Our essayists have written on issues such as Brexit, identity politics, the Irish abroad, the refugee crisis, the need for solidarity and compassion in our societal and global relations, and on so many other matters that underlie, propel, or illustrate that greatest of conflicts facing our society today – that of individualism versus collectivism.

Hubert Butler realised that it is through the building of communities that are ethical in their structure and practice that we create the inclusive and ethical societies on which a truly equal and just world can be founded.

In his work, Butler constantly alludes to that which fractures communities, which subjugates a sense of shared humanity in favour of strident forms of nationalism and populism. The most critical of these fissures is resentment of those perceived as 'other', a resentment that can so quickly lead to the viewing of one group of fellow citizens as being less than human and to the loss of any sense of shared humanity, which in turn enables a brutality and lack of mercy towards groups of fellow citizens.

We should never forget the price paid by Hubert

Butler himself and his family in terms of ignorance, bigotry, sectarianism, and boycotting. It was a terrible time in our relatively recent history. We must learn from it.

Our essayists, too, in their writings, have made important connections between communities that are ethical in their structure and practice and the equal and just world to which we aspire.

Today we stand at a critical juncture in world history, a time for deepening and extending citizenship and rediscovering instincts of empathy and caring that may have been neglected in favour of extreme forms of individualism. Hubert Butler's daughter, Julia Crampton, has expressed the hope that 'perhaps this year's essays will give us some ideas of what Hubert might have thought of the world today in all its extreme chaos.'

I think she will be greatly pleased by the submissions, which are clearly written by citizens who are prepared to reflect on and explore the questions, the answers, the values, and the actions necessary to lead us towards a shared future built on the spirit of cooperation, high ethical standards and integrity, the collective will, real participation, and an exciting sense of what might be possible.

I will conclude by congratulating this year's winner, Michael Amherst, for his excellent and most interesting reflection on identity politics and how they should operate within the context of the common good. I wish him, and all our entrants, every deserved success in the future.

# Preface

*Roy Foster*

Hubert Butler wrote about dark times, particularly the 1930s, and one of his great contributions was to analyse the way that human beings behave during times of crisis. Above all, he showed an unerring ability to clarify people's attitudes towards others and implicitly towards themselves. The opening words of his essays are invariably striking, but perhaps most arresting is the reflection that begins 'The Kagran Gruppe' (1988):

> I believe one of the happiest times of my life was when I was working for the Austrian Jews in Vienna in 1938–9. It is strange to be happy when others are miserable, but all the people at the Freundeszentrum in the Singerstrasse were cheerful too. The reason surely is that we have always known of the immense unhappiness that all humanity has to suffer. We read of it in the newspapers and hear it on the radio but can do nothing about it.

'Doing something about it' is the theme of the lacerating reminiscence that follows, about helping Jewish families escape from Austria after the Anschluss. Butler skewers the apathy and collaborationism of people who should have known better and gives full due to the Quaker organisations that stepped into the breach. Here, as in essays such as 'The Invader Wore Slippers' and 'The Sub-Prefect Should Have Held His Tongue', the competing claims of individualism (whether independent or self-interested) are balanced against the pressures of group identity and perceived duty to the wider world: a theme that pervades many of his essays on Irish matters too. The issues at stake are not always as clear-cut, nor the times as dark, as in Vienna in 1938. But at the present moment, a time of global crisis and the peddling of dangerously simplistic populist shibboleths, the issue of adherence to personal versus group identity is thrown more power-fully into relief than ever.

These thoughts partly inspired the subject chosen by our Judges' Committee (Catriona Crowe, Nicholas Grene, Eva Hoffman, Barbara Schwepcke, and myself) for the 2020 Hubert Butler Essay Prize: 'Communal solidarity and individual freedom: antagonists or allies?' The implications of the title are far-reaching and cover a wide range of possible tensions and conflicts of inter-est; this was reflected in a large and comprehensive entry.

The competition attracted forty submissions from a wide variety of locations and perspectives. In the end, we were unanimous in awarding the first prize to Michael Amherst for his incisive essay focusing on identity politics and how they operate when several kinds of 'identity' clash – particularly in the case of prioritising access to drugs that ameliorate one kind of condition as opposed to another. Amherst elegantly makes the case that an assertion of individual rights and 'freedom' necessarily involves engagement with the public realm. He invokes thinkers as varied as the Enlightenment philosopher Benjamin Constant, the religious thinker Martin Buber, and the novelist James Baldwin, but argues – appropriately – very much as his own person. In its exploration of how to negotiate 'multiple points of belonging and conflicting interests', as well as its vivid touches of personal experience, his essay delivers the kind of nuanced yet punchy impact that is fully in the spirit of this prize and of Hubert Butler himself.

The impressive runners-up also represented striking and relevant discussions of the prescribed theme. Tara McEvoy, like several others, opened her essay by considering the advocates and opponents of face-coverings during the coronavirus pandemic, and the way that face masks have become 'a symbol of a perceived tension between individual liberties and the necessity of collective action'. Following Dalia Gebrial's redefinition of 'individual freedom' as a necessarily much more comprehensive concept than the limited version embraced by current Western libertarian thought, McEvoy broadens out the discussion to the politics of Brexit and attitudes towards refugees, and the heartening examples of communal solidarity 'facilitat[ing] individual freedom' during the pandemic in Belfast, where she lives. The same message comes through Louis MacNeice's long poem 'Autumn Journal' (written at just the time Hubert Butler was working in Vienna). McEvoy appositely concludes that MacNeice's vision of human struggle is a precursor to Butler's observation in *Escape from the Anthill* that his fellow citizens were 'juggling in different ways with the old human constants which are under threat, neighbourhoods, kinships, beliefs, skills, traditions'.

The other runner-up was David Crane, whose essay throws a wide net, covering refugee settlements in Uganda and Ghana, the contrasting attitudes demonstrated in Turkey by the influx of people from Syria, and the effects of trade liberalisation on agricultural production in sub-Saharan Africa. The decisively internationalist perspective of his essay brought a new dimension to the question posed in the title, and pinpointed critical areas where meanings of 'freedom' require fresh and close interrogation.

All three essays argue for the necessary interdependence between individual freedom and communal solidarity. They do so using different examples, illustrations, and arguments, but all share the ability to hone a personal reflection into a general argument, central to the essay form since Montaigne – and consummately demonstrated by Hubert Butler. The winning essays are also written with a close attention to style, spectacularly characteristic of Butler's oeuvre but sometimes at a discount today. The existence of this essay prize, and the entries it galvanises, is reassuring proof that dark times like those we are experiencing today can be illuminated by the distilled intelligence of a 3,000-word essay, as brilliantly shown by Butler's intellectual searchlight beamed out to the world from the study of Maiden Hall, perched above a Kilkenny river valley. And in their different ways, these essays point towards ways of achieving the strange sense of fulfilment that Hubert Butler so memorably found in the Freundeszentrum in 1938.

# Introduction

*Eva Hoffman*

It was a particular kind of pleasure to be part of the jury (for the second time in my case) of this year's Hubert Butler Essay Prize. The process of deciding on the subject and judging the essays submitted to us took place in highly unusual (although by now all-too-familiar) circumstances: during the Covid-19 crisis and its necessary fragmentation of social ties. It was therefore spirit-lifting to meet with fellow jurors – even in virtual form – and to discuss our shared task in a collegial spirit, which allowed for fruitful disagreement in the process of reaching consensus.

The subject we set for this year's prize perhaps inevitably reflected the concerns foregrounded by this unprecedented situation. The need for solidarity on every level, from the local to the national (and now, increasingly, global) has been evident during the pandemic, but its expressions often required constraints on personal freedom – for example, the wearing of masks, or, in a sharper paradox, accepting a period of isolation for the sake of the collective good.

These matters were on everyone's (or at least on many people's) minds, and there was a risk that the subject we chose was, so to speak, overdetermined, and that the entrants for the prize would naturally turn to the current situation for their material – as some indeed did. But, of course, the relationship between solidarity and freedom is central to our highly diverse democracies – indeed, to our globalised world – at the best, as well as the most critical, of times. Among the forty essays submitted to us, there was a surprising and stimulating variety of subject and approach, as well as thought and principle. There were essays on the Polish 'Solidarity' movement and its replacement by individualist capitalism; on the 'fictive' nature of groups, and the need not only for formal structures but for personal responsibility to hold them together; and on different approaches to refugees, exemplified by their treatment in Bidibidi Refugee Settlement, where they were given maximum liberty to everyone's benefit, and in Turkey, where tensions between the host community and Syrian refugees were exacerbated by the sheer scale of the influx.

The essay is a wonderfully flexible form that can travel from the personal to the political, employ the individual voice to probe abstract ideas, and combine insight into a moment with historical perspective. The best essays submitted to us did this, and also acknowledged not only the interweaving between freedom and solidarity but sometimes the tensions between them. The winning essay, published here with two runners-up and two essays awarded a special mention, is a critique of identity politics that argues forcefully that a 'sectoral' concept of interest, based on a narrowly defined 'identity', undermines the idea of the common good and limits individual freedom. Beginning with his own experience of a difficult illness – an aspect of self that, he argues, would not have been taken into account in campaigns by gay groups for more NHS attention and money – Michael Amherst goes on to quote such diverse thinkers as James Baldwin, Benjamin Constant, Kenan Malik, and Martin Buber, to thought-provoking and relevant effect.

I think Hubert Butler, who was a great internationalist as well as a master essayist, would have been pleased with the variety of places from which this year's submitted essays originated: not only the UK and Ireland but Italy, Australia, Bulgaria, Norway, Bosnia–Herzegovina, Cyprus, and Greece. And I think he would have approved of this year's subject. Butler understood that solidarity is not only an abstract virtue but one of our deepest adult desires – and that we need it, even in less extreme conditions, to enable all members of our societies to achieve conditions of meaningful freedom.

# Michael Amherst

*First Place*

The poet Nick Laird observed in the *New York Review of Books*, 'We already did identity politics in Northern Ireland: it didn't work out so well.' Yet today it seems identity is the fundamental driver of our politics. Our freedoms, our values, our political affiliations, all are intimately tied up with who – or what – we are.

Clearly this has a general, inescapable logic: up until the last century, your right to vote and to hold property would have been determined in large part by your sex; the likelihood of you being enslaved in recent centuries would have been decided by matters of race; the likelihood of your sexual proclivities landing you in trouble with the law would chiefly have been determined by whether your partner was the same sex as yourself. However, while a focus on identity may have helped minority groups secure freedoms denied us, arguably it has done so at the cost of individual freedom, as well as social cohesion. To focus on what differentiates us diminishes a sense of a communal solidarity founded in our shared humanity. As Laird went on, 'the rest of the world turned into Northern Ireland: partisan, oppositional, identity-focused.'

I was reminded of this a couple of years ago at the height of a campaign by gay men in the UK for the health service to fund PrEP (or pre-exposure prophylaxis). PrEP prevents the transmission of HIV infection without the need for a condom. However, it does not protect against other STIs and, at the time, cost £4,800 per person a year.

I was thirty-five years old and could hardly walk. I suffer from psoriatic arthritis, the same autoimmune condition that plagued Dennis Potter and famously featured in his work *The Singing Detective*. Each morning, I would wake stiff and in severe pain. It would take a good half hour or so to get out of bed, bent over, with my head almost between my legs, before I'd shuffle to the bathroom. There, I would have a long hot bath, instead of a shower, as heat has been shown to ease morning stiffness. Sometimes it would take me a while to struggle back out of the bath, and then I would contend with dressing myself, unable to reach my feet to put on my socks, unable to manage the mobility required to get my arms into my shirtsleeves. On the worst days, it could be three hours before I was able to leave the house. At the time, my doctors were waiting for funding approval for a new drug, one they hoped would suppress my immune system and render my symptoms non-existent.

Few issues so starkly illustrate conflicts between the freedom of the individual and the public good than health, as experience of the coronavirus has shown. With a limited budget, the NHS will always have to juggle an array of competing demands. To my ear, the campaign for PrEP was deaf to this fact, deaf to the other calls upon NHS funding and the need to situate its argument within this context.

Representative of the tone of the campaign, and the many opinion pieces, was one by the *Guardian* columnist Owen Jones, with the headline 'The NHS must show it cares about gay men's lives – and roll out PrEP HIV drugs'. Rather than making the argument solely about why PrEP should be funded, its necessity, and its efficacy relative to other treatments, Jones and others claimed that the very identity of those campaigning was what made its cause worthy of support. By making the issue one of freedom and rights, campaigners made it personal and claimed a degree of exceptionalism relative to others.

Individuals and minority groups need to engage with public discourse to advocate for our rights. In his novel *Adolphe*, the philosopher Benjamin Constant explores the risks for the individual who tries to live outside the public sphere. Drawing upon the argument made in his lecture 'The Liberty of Ancients Compared with that of Moderns', Constant argues that 'moderns' cannot lead a solely private life of individual freedom. To live truly privately, to have real individual freedom, paradoxically one must engage with the public realm, if only to protect the privacy one values. James Baldwin understood this, saying that his novel *Giovanni's Room* 'made a public announcement that we're private, if you see what I mean.'

Identity politics has been very good at securing rights, but less so when situating them within the common good. The campaign for gay marriage was a rare exception, framing its argument around the idea that all love and relationships should hold equal weight. The danger is identity politics finds solace in a narrower sphere than the communal. Individuals find comfort and solidarity only with their own kind. These groups and their characteristics become ever smaller, ever more atomised (look at the growing plethora of letters in 'LGBT+'), but never to the point of focusing on the particular, the individual. This way, the communal is reduced to the sectarian. Yet wider communal society doesn't disappear.

As Constant knew, the public must be engaged with. On an episode of *Question Time* at the start of 2020, Laurence Fox argued with an audience member over whether the treatment of Meghan Markle by the UK press was racist. The audience member, a woman of colour, challenged his assertion that the UK is not racist because Fox is 'a white, privileged male' and therefore had not experienced the same kind of discrimination. This was met with widespread groans from the audience. However, there was no indication the audience agreed with Fox's assertion – they just resented the attempt to close down debate. Rather than explaining why Fox was wrong, how the treatment of Markle is different from the treatment of white celebrities or royals, the questioner used identity as a means of refusing further dialogue.

As Constant argued in his lecture and demonstrated in the character of Adolphe, we will have to have these arguments anyway. A politics of identity that finds strength in the artificial security of a sectoral solidarity ignores this reality. It expects its values to be translated to the communal but without the dialogue or work that drives social change.

This results in a society atomised into competing sectoral interests. By making the argument in favour of PrEP about the rights of a particular group, campaigners immediately pitted themselves against other groups also waiting for drug funding. The language became about a hierarchy of need and privilege. I felt myself more deserving than a gay man wanting PrEP because the drug I needed was not about choice and merely preventative but would enable me to walk, yet a cystic fibrosis sufferer was arguably more deserving than either of us because the drug they were waiting for would enable them to live for longer.

The consequence of a focus on identity over consensus is a politics that is wholly individualistic and ignores the needs of others. In criminal justice, the individual wants of the victim and perpetrator are subordinated to the (perceived) greater objectivity of the community. However, identity politics does not allow for this. Instead, our sense of solidarity with others and trust in the community is secondary to our individual place in an imperfect hierarchy of difference and resultant grievance. Yet the rights and freedoms of the individual can only be secured by consent. The individual has to recognise their place and duty to the wider community, just as the community must to the individual.

One pernicious consequence of the left's adoption of identity politics has been the far right's rebranding of racism as white identity politics. However, one could view this as inevitable: if you tell people that their only route to a hearing is to emphasise their identity, or in some instances that their identity is what denies them a hearing, then why are we surprised if those who feel persecuted, forgotten, and sidelined feel the need to assert their difference as the only means of being heard?

Identity politics disenfranchises those – particularly the poor and weak – who cannot brandish one of the limited appropriate identity traits as qualification.

Phoebe Maltz Bovy takes this further in *The Perils of 'Privilege'*, observing how the language of privilege creates conditions in which people are forced to reveal things about themselves in order to gain a hearing. If society mandates that only those with a certain identity or experience are able to speak to certain issues – the phenomenon of 'speaking as a...' – then only those who reveal all aspects of themselves are qualified to speak. Furthermore, this creates a hierarchy in which the validity of an argument is predicated on what you are, rather than what you say.

Wherever one stands in relation to the furore over J. K. Rowling and trans rights, there is surely something invidious about a situation in which a woman feels forced to reveal her status as a survivor of domestic violence in order to qualify her right to speak on the issue of women's refuges and spaces. For advocates of free speech and free expression, a reasonable question in this instance might be: in what circumstances should J. K. Rowling's views be heard? For some, it would seem the answer is: never.

The foundations of identity politics are themselves reductive. Baldwin claimed, 'There's nothing in me that is not in everybody else, and nothing in everybody else that is not in me.' However, naming people based on an attribute – their gender, their race, their sexuality – rejects our shared humanity in favour of an objectifying otherness. This speaks to its origins in the reactionary right. As the writer and academic Kenan Malik observes, 'The original politics of identity was that of racial difference, the insistence that one's racial identity determines one's moral and social place in the world.'

And yet, there are those who would wish to counter Baldwin: that there definitely is something in me, not in you; that what I share is shared only with a select group; that my identity characteristics make me special. For advocates of identity politics to elevate their group identity over communal solidarity is to concede the very ground reactionaries use to oppress. It undermines our claim to equality while also undermining our solidarity with others.

The freedom of identity politics is a reduced one, one that comes at a loss of complexity in favour of specific identity traits. It presumes that anyone in this 'group' shares the same experience of oppression and thus the same aims. Your sectoral solidarity trumps your individual complexity. To fail to conform with all aspects of sectoral dogma is taken as evidence not of the failure or limits of such a politics but of a lack of allyship or false consciousness on your part.

When I disagreed with the tactics of the PrEP campaign, in spite of being a bisexual man, I was accused of being a traitor to the cause. Yet in response to cries that the NHS needed to show it cared about the health of men who have sex with men, I could have replied, 'Well, yes it can, by giving me drugs that will allow me to walk.' Which men, I wondered, was the NHS meant to care about? The gay men who'd watched their loved ones die in the AIDS pandemic, now entering old age and needing greater medical interventions themselves? Gay men in need of cancer drugs? Or the gay man terrified for the future of his nephew suffering from cystic fibrosis, unable to get treatment that will keep him alive because the NHS deemed it too expensive?

Identity politics is a form of predestination in which our actions are predetermined by our group membership. Perversely, your actions are secondary to your identity: what you do matters far less than what you are. Yet failure to accord with your group challenges your legitimacy within it. Being a man who has sex with men is not enough; you are expected to hold certain positions and ideals too. Otherwise, you can be labelled a 'fake gay', like tech billionaire Peter Thiel. Or, as Joe Biden said to an interviewer, 'If you have a problem figuring out whether you're for me or Trump, then you ain't black.'

My error was holding the 'wrong' view, one that did

not accord with my group belonging. But then again, I arguably did have the right view to accord with my membership of a group of disabled people. This is the point: each of us is made up of multiple points of belonging and conflicting interests. What of the individual whose identities contradict? Or whose wishes don't intersect? Identity politics does not allow for these complexities. It erases our particularity, while demanding we adhere to a limited groupthink.

Who is really free in such a scenario, in which what you do no longer matters, your actions are unimportant, because what you do is dictated by what you are? If the price of your limited freedom is to have your humanity reduced to a series of traits that determine your values and actions, then you are not free. It denies agency. It's determinist and limited, and has origins in far-right discrimination, seeing individuals only as the product of their caste.

Part of the mistake is the equating of solidarity with accord, or sameness. We can be united around a cause yet hold a variety of differing views and values. For example, in the United States, the Prison Rape Elimination Act (PREA) was passed with unanimous congressional support – unprecedented in recent US history. It was sponsored in the Senate by the Republican Jeff Sessions and the Democrat Ted Kennedy, and supported by evangelical Christian Republicans as well as left-wing, socialist Democrats. Their values and aims were diametrically opposed, but they all agreed that rape in prison was bad. Just Detention International, the human rights organisation that led the campaign for PREA, managed such unanimity by focusing on common principles and goals, as opposed to the identities of the parties concerned.

Yet how do individuals and groups secure their rights, their freedoms, in such a way that does not antagonise the wider community? An unlikely place for a better alternative is Martin Buber's work *I and Thou*, which emphasises both the universal and the particular. Buber argues that most of the time our experience of the world, and each other, is that of subject and object, or an 'I-and-It' relationship. However, what we should aspire to is a relationship of 'I-and-Thou', one that *meets* the other. Many have struggled to define what Buber means in a way that is not still relational, that doesn't fall into the language of subject and object. One way might be to regard it as a dynamic relationship – both dynamic and *a* dynamic, in that it is an encounter that changes all concerned. This can be observed in practice when opposing sides are brought together to meet their antagonists, rather than merely dealing in abstract argument. For example, a shift in attitudes towards gay people has come with greater visibility and engagement with gay lives.

Part of Buber's premise is echoed in Catholic theology: that we are all equal in the eyes of God, while also all being unique. This results in the interesting paradox of a universalism coupled with the particular. It is about a call for equality across identity lines – for those lines seed difference and exceptionalism – and a recognition that difference comes at the individual level.

Politics is forced to speak in a language of generalisations. However, a language that is grounded in I-and-Thou refuses to objectify; it does not reduce people to categories or presumed special interests, instead recognising that we all have particularities of experience, of pasts, of present advantages and difficulties, and will handle them differently. It sees all of us as part of a universal whole, entitled to the same rights and freedoms. To reduce you or me to an attribute erases our particularity; it denies that all of our stories are different. If I-and-Thou affirms difference, it is at the level that we are all different – it meets me as I am, in all my complex contradictions. Identity politics results in communities that are fractured, partisan, oppositional. The freedom it secures is a limited one grounded in the very objectification that foments discrimination. It does not seek to convince or persuade; it rejects allies and seeks antagonists.

Ultimately, its conception of who and what we are is limited. When we think of who we are, it is likely that we will think of both our close, intimate ties – even those individual traits peculiar to us – as well as our place in the wider world. Sitting here at home right now, I'm mulling news of my mother's advancing cancer. I remember being told as a child, 'You are your mother's son,' which I took to mean I had her eyes, her colouring, and, probably, her tendency to the dramatic. I also remember being told, 'You are your father's son,' which I took to mean I clearly liked a drink, or my eyes shone as I was about to make a joke at someone's expense. Right now, these are the traits that feel meaningful to me.

None of us are siloed into only one form of general group belonging. I'm also a writer, I think of myself as on the political left, I'm a child of the West Country, I live in London, I'm a citizen of the UK and Europe. All of these traces, particular and individual to me, exist within a context, within a wider community. I cannot forget my duty to that community, a duty that includes advocating for the freedom of myself and others within it. I can only be sure of my community's solidarity with me by committing myself to it, by remaining in dialogue with others. They understand this in Northern Ireland, and they learned the hard way.

# Tara McEvoy

*Runner-up*

On 14 July 2020, Conservative MP Desmond Swayne stood in the House of Commons and delivered a tirade against new plans to make face masks mandatory in some public places, an incentive to slow the spread of Covid-19, to 'flatten the curve' of the virus's infection rate. 'Nothing,' he emphasised, 'would make me less likely to go shopping than the thought of having to mask up.' The requirement to do so, he argued, would be a 'monstrous imposition against me and a number of outraged and reluctant constituents.' Swayne's protestations were out of line with majority public opinion in the UK at that time: 91 per cent of Britons thought wearing masks should be compulsory on public transport; 80 per cent thought the same for shops; 68 per cent thought masks should be mandatory in busy outdoor areas. But the MP wasn't alone in his criticism of 'having to mask up'. Brexit Party leader Nigel Farage, typically facetious, told *Politico* that the demand for members of the public to wear masks made him want to 'stick two fingers up and shout abusive language at the television.' At the end of the month, in the North of Ireland, Democratic Unionist Party MP Sammy Wilson tweeted a photo of himself in an ice cream parlour, unmasked and smiling, bearing the caption 'Support local business. You can't eat [ice cream] when you're muzzled!' And this was just what was happening in the UK. From country to country, different versions of the same debate were playing out. In Germany, individual states were given the power to impose their own rules on mask-wearing; in France, every shop owner could decide for themselves whether to make mask-wearing mandatory on their premises. Since it had started appearing everywhere from the supermarket to the train station, the face mask had rapidly become a symbol of ideology, a symbol of a perceived tension between individual liberties and the necessity of collective action.

In this respect, the face mask has epitomised something of the broader debate surrounding the response of individual countries to the coronavirus pandemic. How much personal freedom would each citizen be willing to relinquish, temporarily, in the interests of the public good? What sacrifices were too great? What could people bear, and for how long? The day after Swayne made his remarks in the Commons, I was making dinner and, in the background, put on an episode of Novara Media's current affairs YouTube show *Tysky-Sour*, my laptop perched on a box of Cheerios laid flat on the kitchen counter. The host, Michael Walker, was discussing the political refusal to wear masks with John McDonnell's former advisor James Meadway and Dalia Gebrial, an LSE academic. Walker, speaking from the Novara studio, argued that the UK face mask debate verged on silly – that it was a distraction from the real issues of the day – but then Gebrial started speaking about how the stakes were actually very high indeed. I turned down the heat on the hob, let the tomato sauce I was making simmer, and turned to watch the screen as she put into words everything that was revealed by this refusal, in terms I have been thinking about since:

> It reflects these very narrow and individualised ideas of freedom that have really governed the West in particular since the rise of neoliberalism ... It kind of looks at individual behaviour as only relevant or only important insofar as individually borne consequences. It doesn't consider how perhaps minor concessions, or behaviours that may be minor to one person, could have significant impacts on the collective freedom – the idea that we are not just individuals existing in our little silos but actually our behaviour impacts on

the collective good. That's one thing this pandemic has really challenged. You don't just have to think about your likelihood of getting the virus, or the consequences for you if you're exposed to the virus ... but think about being a vector, potentially transmitting it.

A vector: a single individual touching a whole network. For Gebrial, the argument struck at a key tenet of modern-day Western politics: it displayed how individualism had been valorised (there being, in the infamous words of Margaret Thatcher, 'no such thing as society'), how acting in the public good had been 'portrayed as a weakness'. It has, and continues to be: we see it in everything from the popularity of Bear Grylls – one man battling against the vastness and violence of nature – to the election of Donald Trump and the increasing populism of the political sphere, as other 'big personalities', 'television characters', take aim at the very *idea* of collective governance. We see it in an incessant media focus on people over policies. Arguably, we might read individual exceptionalism as a motivation behind the Brexit vote, too, influenced as it was by the rhetoric of 'going our own way', 'taking back control'.

The same isolationist rhetoric was peddled out once again in the summer of 2020 as the refugee crisis intensified – those desperate people on boats and dinghies unable to simply 'pull themselves up by the bootstraps' – and as Britain responded by appointing a 'Clandestine Channel Threat Commander' to make their sea journeys to UK shores 'unviable' – a stroke of astonishing cruelty. As we entered the first lockdown, the acceptability – the valorisation – of radical individualism as a worldview, as a basis for behaviour, had resulted in supermarket shelves lying bare, stripped of essential produce as individuals rushed to shore up individual supplies, as we all rushed to safeguard 'our little silos'.

On the Novara YouTube discussion show, Gebrial spoke, too, about the groups who were more seriously affected by a widespread ambivalence towards mask-wearing: older people, disabled people, those with underlying conditions. And it is true, of course, that different groups have experienced this crisis differently. In addition to those aforementioned, we might add people of colour, who, in the UK, have been disproportionately likely to contract coronavirus; working-class people, including those for whom it was impossible to work from home during the strictest phases of lockdown; and, abroad, people in countries with poor or privatised healthcare systems. For all the rhetoric of everyone 'being in this together', these divisions continue to make themselves felt. To paraphrase Orwell, we are all equal, but some are more equal than others. As the pandemic progresses, I have been routinely reminded of Friedrich Engels' book *The Condition of the Working Class in England*, this passage in particular:

> When one individual inflicts bodily injury upon another such that death results, we call the deed manslaughter; when the assailant knew in advance that the injury would be fatal, we call his deed murder. But when society places hundreds of proletarians in such a position that they inevitably meet a too early and an unnatural death, one which is quite as much a death by violence as that by the sword or bullet; when it deprives thousands of the necessaries of life, places them under conditions in which they cannot live ... its deed is murder just as surely as the deed of the single individual.

What does freedom mean in this context? When we now act without communal solidarity, *who* gets to be free? Who remains oppressed; whose oppression is *deepened*? These questions were largely ignored in the UK as the government first dallied over acting to stop the spread of coronavirus, and then scrambled to piece together an adequate response, all too little too late. As in many other countries, public messaging on the pandemic response here has deliberately lacked clarity. While it has been heartening to see mutual aid groups seek to fill the void left by the government's inaction, it's enraging that they should have had to do so in the first place. In Belfast, where I live, as in many other cities across the UK and Ireland, a rising number of coronavirus cases in early March was met with an outpouring of neighbourly sentiment – and a good deal of practical help amongst neighbours. On Facebook, groups formed where people posted offers to go grocery shopping for people in their area, or pick up medicine for those who couldn't make it out of the house. Posters volunteering assistance appeared in windows. A local art gallery and framing shop closed down and, in their newly imposed free time, its owner and workers started a soup kitchen, delivering meals daily around the city. Here was communal solidarity being used to *facilitate* individual freedom: the more responsibly everyone in the community acted, the safer – the freer – the most vulnerable would be. When the number of cases fell by enough, those shielding would be able to go outside again; we would all be able to see our loved ones again.

A couple of months into the first lockdown, stuck in the house, I read an interview with a Belfast-based artist, Jennifer Mehigan, on the art website *AQNB*. In it, she speaks about mutual aid, models for community care, and the prevalence of these models in certain queer communities:

Even the act of just caring for each other in times of crisis is so familiar in parts of the queer community and it was kind of nuts to watch people bury themselves into surviving as this individual thing and not looking to see who needed something more than them, but I guess that is the fun side of capitalism as always.

That was the other side of the coin: the logic of capitalism – the way in which market interests function as absolute priorities in our society – had become starkly, grimly apparent in the past few months, perhaps more so than ever before during the course of my lifetime, with those market interests pitted directly against public health. The same calculation at every stage of the pandemic: lives versus profit margins, public opinion tipping the balance slightly, the balance tipped back again by a relentless media campaign. Boris Johnson and Michael Gove and Priti Patel grinning, pulling pints behind the bar at a Wetherspoons as the death toll creeps steadily upwards. Rishi Sunak encouraging everyone to have a meal in their local Wagamama franchise. Freshly applied stickers on every shop window: *Welcome home! We've missed you!* A strange kind of freedom, a cost unevenly divided.

*

As summer wore on, as the race for a vaccine sped along, I returned to the poetry of Louis MacNeice. I had written a Master's dissertation on his work a few years ago; I spent the summer working long shifts at a sandwich bar in a town an hour away, getting the bus to Belfast, heading straight to the library to find critical texts on his collections. It had been a frantic season, but my fondness for his work hadn't diminished – there's something profoundly reassuring about his voice. He's the friend you'd call before a job interview, or after a break-up, or in the midst of a global pandemic, say. I reread *Autumn Journal*, the book-length poem MacNeice wrote between August and December 1938, as the world was on the brink of war. In correspondence with T. S. Eliot, his editor at Faber & Faber, MacNeice called the poem 'a panorama and a confession of faith'. If he has faith in anything, it's people:

> And Aristotle was right to posit the Alter Ego
> But wrong to make it only a halfway house:
> Who could expect – or want – to be spiritually
>     self-supporting,
> Eternal self-abuse?
> Why not admit that other people are always
> Organic to the self, that a monologue
> Is the death of language and that a single lion
> Is less himself, or alive, than a dog and another dog?

For the dissertation, I'd been writing about the tension between individualism and collectivism in his work, and in the margins of my copy of his *Collected Poems* were my workings out, little notes on my readings: *atomised individualism, totalitarianism??, the ethics of A. J.??, no man is an island etc.* I'd been bogged down with terminology, with political philosophy, with trying to say something clever; I could have spent more time just sitting with the poems, stewing on them. When I did now, I was struck again – more powerfully – by MacNeice's humanity. He's deeply invested in individual freedom, deeply suspicious of the totalitarian regimes gaining strength across Europe at the time of his writing, but he realises that the freedom of the individual is predicated on collective efforts: 'Why not admit that other people are always / Organic to the self'? As Charles Taylor would later put it, in his 1991 philosophical treatise *The Ethics of Authenticity*,

> We are expected to develop our own opinions, outlook, stances to things, to a considerable degree through solitary reflection. But this is not how things work with important issues, such as the definition of our identity. We define this always in dialogue with, sometimes in struggle against, the identities our significant others want to recognize in us.

Our significant others: the others who are significant to us, for us.

'And I think with joy how whatever, now or in the future, the system / Nothing whatever can take / The people away, there will always be people / For friends or lovers' writes MacNeice; there will always be others, becoming significant. This includes those 'others' Mac-Neice encounters in a besieged Barcelona, 'ripe as an egg for revolt and ruin', as he travels there and learns about the suffering of the Spanish people under fascism. The 'peasants', the poor, the children begging in the streets: all these people *organic to the self*. The realisation instils a sense of duty in the poet: 'The nicest people in England have always been the least / Apt to solidarity or alignment / But all of them must now align against the beast / That prowls at every door and barks in every headline.' The rise of fascism in Spain isn't just a distant issue for MacNeice: it threatens the freedom of individuals across Europe, across the *world*. Responsibility to one's fellow citizens doesn't end at any shoreline. A collective, pan-European, *international* fight against fascism is the only viable approach. Communal solidarity is a political necessity.

What would MacNeice make of 2020, this strange and terrible year? We'll never know, but *Autumn Journal* provides some clue. The poem begins with a kind of slowly dawning horror, similar to that which engulfed the world in the early months of this year, but it ends on a note of optimism, shock giving way to a resolve to make it through, to do better. MacNeice asks that we 'pray for a possible land / Not of sleep-walkers, not of angry puppets / But where both heart and brain can understand / The movements of our fellows'; a land where 'nobody sees the use / Of buying money and blood at the cost of blood and money, / Where the individual, no longer squandered / In self-assertion, works with the rest.' Some years later, in 1985's *Escape from the Anthill*, Hubert Butler would observe that his fellow citizens were 'juggling in different ways with the old human constants which are under threat, neighbourhoods, kinships, beliefs, skills, traditions'. The same 'juggling' is explored in MacNeice's writing; the same juggling continues at the present moment.

Today, the biggest challenges facing us – from coronavirus to longer-standing societal crises such as racism, classism, sexism, and the climate crisis – simply *cannot* be overcome by people acting on an individual basis. Rather, collective action is a necessary precondition of individual freedom. We might think, here, of the many individual freedoms that have been won *due to* collective action, communal solidarity: from sexual and reproductive rights to legislative protections for minorities. An intersectional approach to activism has benefitted groups working towards the same eventual ends; as Audre Lorde once famously declared, 'I am not free while any woman is unfree, even when her shackles are very different from my own.' To interpret, broadly, the title of Joe Hill's 1913 leftist anthem, 'There Is Power in a Union', is to recognise the essential importance of people *working together* towards common goals.

This isn't to say that individuals can't make a difference. History shows us that they can, and often do. Emma Goldman, Jim Larkin, Claudette Colvin, Rosa Parks, Steve Biko, Nelson Mandela, Simone Veil, Malcolm X, Martin Luther King Jr., Fred Hampton, Angela Davis, Marsha P. Johnson, Sylvia Rivera, Bernadette Devlin, Ailbhe Smyth, Harvey Milk, Malala Yousafzai, Greta Thunberg, Emma González: the list goes on. But history also shows us that solidarity between different people, different groups, is ultimately what's needed for liberation. It's not a question of flattening those differences, of calling on people to suspend critical thought or personal imagination, of instilling a kind of 'mob mentality', but of *harnessing* difference in the service of something greater.

The writer and activist Sarah Schulman speaks about this in an interview with *Slate* broadcasted shortly after the death of controversial playwright Larry Kramer. Both were involved in the organisation ACT UP, the grassroots political group that worked to end the AIDS pandemic, but each took vastly different approaches to their activism. For Schulman, this capacity for dissent was one of the chief strengths of the organisation: 'One of the questions that people have about ACT UP is why was it successful? ... One of the answers to that is that ACT UP was a group that did not rely on consensus and allowed for simultaneity of response.' Speaking to a very different context (mid-twentieth-century Irish censorship), Francis Hackett, a writer who was, like Butler, a Kilkenny native, described it like this in the 1936 *Dublin Magazine* essay 'A Muzzle Made in Ireland': 'multiplicity-in-unity ... is the supreme hope for the development of the individual.' Solidarity has extraordinary consequences for individual lives – it *saves* individual lives. When we act without it, we allow the worst inequalities of our society to go unchecked, to persist, to intensify. When we act with it, we realise MacNeice's vision of a future where the individual, no longer squandered in self-assertion, works with the rest to the benefit of everyone.

# David Crane

*Runner-up*

During the summer of 2018, whilst conducting monitoring and evaluation for a small refugee-focused charity, I visited Bidibidi Refugee Settlement, located in Yumbe District, northern Uganda. Until August 2016, Bidibidi was a small and exceptionally normal village, indistinguishable from any other in Yumbe. However, following a dramatic intensification of violence in South Sudan, where civil war had been waged since 2013, refugee inflows increased exponentially, and Uganda's existing refugee-hosting infrastructure became fiercely overburdened. This led to the conception of what was, just five months later, the world's largest refugee settlement: Bidibidi Refugee Settlement. Given the extraordinary strain bestowed upon this rural and underdeveloped village, one would be forgiven for assuming a rapid decay in local infrastructure and livelihoods. But, on the contrary, the reality that I witnessed was quite the opposite. The settlement, as well as the surrounding area, was markedly distinct from the neighbouring villages. Elements of substantial urbanisation were clear, with investment from the government of Uganda, international non-governmental organisations (INGOs), and private enterprises enjoying a significant presence: government health facilities, UN Refugee Agency schools, and Orange [the mobile network operator] radio towers were all commonplace, to name just a few examples.

My observations of Bidibidi are reminiscent of writings on the Buduburam Refugee Camp in southern Ghana, opened to host Liberian refugees during the 1990s, which has been described as undergoing a dramatic transformation from a small rural village into a thriving urban centre, possessing many luxuries which were more typically confined to Ghana's major cities, such as internet cafes and tarmacked roads (Omata, 2017).* Theoretically, the rapid economic development experienced in cases such as Bidibidi and Buduburam has been interpreted as a consequence of the successful allyship between communal solidarity and individual freedom. Case studies reveal the striking lengths that host communities and refugees alike have gone to in order to ensure mutual empowerment and prosperity.

---

* N. Omata, *The Myth of Self-Reliance: Economic Lives Inside A Liberian Refugee Camp*, (n.p., 2017).

For instance, in Yumbe, members of the local host communities donated significant portions of their land to enable refugees to practise subsistence farming. Likewise, during periods when food aid provided to refugees was decreased, local hosts generously contributed their crops to reduce incidents of food insecurity.

At the same time, government policies that enabled substantial individual freedoms for refugees have been vital in facilitating a mutually beneficial relationship between the two groups, which has, in turn, produced the thriving economies that can be witnessed today. For example, in both present-day Uganda and in Ghana during the 1990s, refugees enjoy(ed) freedom of movement as well as the right to work. Such policies are rare within less developed countries hosting large numbers of refugees, due to fears of labour market saturation and security concerns. However, the two aforementioned cases provide evidence in strong opposition of such assertions. Allowing refugees to enter the labour market where they can be most productive increases their expenditure in local markets, and many choose to start their own businesses – some of which hire local nationals. Refugees have also been cited as a cheap source of labour for local entrepreneurs, ensuring that gaps in local labour markets have been filled.

However, the findings of Bidibidi and Buduburam

have not been emulated universally; take, for instance, the Turkish response to the Syrian refugee crisis. The Syrian civil war commenced in 2011 and has produced the largest refugee crisis of the twenty-first century. As of August 2020, there are over 5 million Syrians displaced across the globe, and Turkey hosts by far the largest portion – the figure currently stands at around 3.6 million. And, whilst the previously discussed legal freedoms remain present for refugees who seek asylum in Turkey, such as freedom of movement and the right to work, as the number of refugees has risen, there has been a clear breakdown in the communal solidarity that has been practised between host communities and Syrian refugees. Academic studies by the likes of Tumen (2016) and Altındağ et al. (2020) have documented dramatic price increases in local markets; intense increases in labour market competition, which have escalated unemployment amongst both host communities and refugees; and the deterioration of social relationships between the two groups, with incidents of violent clashes becoming increasingly common.*

---

* S. Tumen, 'The Economic Impact of Syrian Refugees on Host Countries: Quasi-experimental Evidence from Turkey', *American Economic Review*, 106/5 (2016), 456–460; O. Altindag, O. Bakis, and S. Rozo, 'Blessing or Burden? Impacts of Refugees on Businesses and the Informal Economy', *Journal of Development Economics*, 146 (2020).

Thus, the question stands, why have host communities and Syrian refugees in Turkey lacked the perfect allyship of communal solidarity and individual freedom described above, seen in Bidibidi and Buduburam? It appears that the granting of individual freedoms to Syrian refugees has, in fact, antagonised the communal solidarity between the host communities and the refugee groups, since the fears of labour market saturation have been realised, and local markets for goods and services have become overwhelmed by the demand shocks presented by the rapidly increasing population. The central thesis of this essay is to argue that the appearance of antagonism between communal solidarity and individual freedom is an illusion, as a result of a surface-level understanding of individual freedom which is too often applied within policy and scholarly arguments. More specifically, individual freedom tends to be understood through a rather privileged lens: the legal right to practise a particular action is falsely equated to the individual freedom to conduct such an action.

Take, for instance, the seminal work of Indian economist and Nobel laureate Amartya Sen, *Development as Freedom*. The fundamental takeaway from the 1999 work is that in order to achieve economic development (primarily in the world's poorest countries) we must expand the basic freedoms available to the average citizen. Such freedoms include access to clean water, health services, and education. These assertions are difficult to contest and have remained widely undisputed in the two decades since the work was published. More controversially, however, Sen also advocates for economic freedoms largely in line with neoliberal economic thought – for instance, the elimination of subsidies and the removal of international trade barriers such as tariffs. Whilst such policies represent a legal expansion of economic freedom which could, in turn, be construed as an expansion of individual freedom granted to citizens, the institution of such policies has time and again been shown to dramatically constrain labour market opportunities and – subsequently – limit other individual freedoms (such as access to education and healthcare). This is particularly true for the most vulnerable members of society.

To illustrate this point, consider trade liberalisation within the agricultural sector in sub-Saharan Africa under structural adjustment programmes during the 1980s. By opening African businesses up to global markets, farmers' economic freedom was theoretically (and legally) expanded. However, the benefits of this 'expansion' were tightly constrained to those holding significantly advanced technologies which enabled their production to be competitively viable against the newly found competition. In contrast, the vast majority of agricultural workers suffered as the demand for their products fell, replaced by demand for cheaper substitutes imported from more technologically advanced nations. What's more, richer agriculturists who benefitted from the reforms increased their demand for land, which in many cases meant that more marginalised farmers (who were negatively impacted) could no longer afford to rent the land that they had previously used for their own agricultural activities. Subsequently, their income fell dramatically, and they also experienced a shrinking of their other individual freedoms, such as access to education for their children (as they could no longer afford the fees).

Returning to the discussion of Turkey, it is clear that the legal freedoms afforded to refugees have not materialised into a real expansion of individual freedoms for the majority of those who have fled the civil war and, as a result, potential mutually beneficial relationships with local host communities have not come to fruition; in fact, the majority of individuals in both groups have faced negative consequences. Regarding the legal right to work granted to Syrian refugees, several inhibiting factors have produced adverse labour market effects. For instance, cultural differences between Syrians and their Turkish hosts have produced difficulties in obtaining employment opportunities. This has meant that the qualifications that refugees obtained in Syria prior to the civil war are not valid within the Turkish labour market. Furthermore, the language barrier presents a major obstacle for gaining employment – particularly 'skilled' employment. Cultural differences are less of an issue in cases such as Ghana and Uganda because of their colonial histories: during the 'scramble for Africa' in the late nineteenth century, colonial powers arbitrarily designated land amongst themselves, resulting in high levels of cultural cohesion between African states – particularly in areas surrounding a country's borders, which is, for the sake of convenience, where refugee settlements tend to be constructed.

Thus, the vast majority of Syrian refugees have been forced into so-called unskilled labour, where they earn wages far below the typical wages for Turkish nationals – reports even indicate that receiving wages in the form of food or clothing is not uncommon. Not only does this mean that refugees are earning disturbingly low wages and failing to make use of their human capital but it means that lower-skilled Turkish nationals have also been forced out of the labour market, and unemployment rates have soared. Witnessing (and in many cases personally experiencing) such events, many Turkish nationals have become disillusioned with their nation's relatively progressive attitudes and policies towards refugees. In turn, communal solidarity has broken down and been replaced by widespread incidents of discrimination and xenophobia.

These unsavoury attitudes have been reinforced by narratives produced by the Turkish government. High-profile politicians including the interior minister, Süleyman Soylu, have spoken out passionately against the 'refugee problem' facing Turkey. Frequently, Syrians are presented as lazy and dependent and, in some cases, downright dangerous; they have become the nation's most common scapegoat and a talking point to gain political notoriety. Such narratives have bred a toxic environment of distrust and discontent towards refugees. Not only has this exacerbated the public's negative attitudes, making it more difficult for Syrians to participate in the labour market (and, in turn, to practise their individual freedom to gain employment) but it has also dramatically reduced the desire to act in solidarity with refugees.

Whilst the actions of the Turkish government (as well as the xenophobic attitudes and actions of the public) are unjustifiable, it is important to note that the issue goes far beyond the decisions and speeches of national politicians. International cooperation within the global refugee regime is notoriously poor. Whilst the 1951 Refugee Convention prohibits the forcible returning of individuals to a country where they face danger and/

or persecution, there are no legally binding commitments to the sharing of the financial costs and physical hosting requirements associated with the flight of refugees – typically (and rather insensitively) referred to as refugee 'burden sharing'. Between 2012 and 2016, the Turkish government spent over US$10 billion in costs associated with hosting Syrian refugees, and yet received just US$450 million in support from the international community. Therefore, when critiquing the Turkish government for its response to the refugee crisis, it is also necessary to extend such criticisms to the international community, which has failed to ensure adequate resources have been available to uphold the individual freedoms of both the refugees and the local host communities.

The problem of 'unskilled' labour market saturation has been intensified by the speed and size of refugee flows into Turkey – as previously mentioned, Syria's civil war has produced the largest refugee crisis of the twenty-first century, and thus the numbers are far greater than those hosted in both Ghana and Uganda. However, the issue is deepened as a result of the settlement patterns practised by the refugees: although they do have the legal right to freedom of movement across Turkey, the vast majority of refugees have settled in just a few large cities including Istanbul, Gaziantep, and Şanlıurfa.

This, again, points to a gap between legal freedoms afforded to refugees and the individual freedoms that they are able to practise in reality. This is partly (and, arguably, largely) because of government and INGO presence. Because of the aforementioned issues associated with obtaining a liveable wage, the vast majority of refugees are dependent on aid from either the Turkish government or charitable organisations such as the UN Refugee Agency. However, to benefit from such aid provisions, refugees are forced to remain in densely populated cities, since the provisions have failed to penetrate into smaller cities and rural regions. Consequently, once again, refugees cannot fully exercise their legal right to freedom of movement, as they are constrained by the actions of outside parties.

Finally, Syrian refugees in Turkey are legally permitted to use social services, including education and health facilities. But, as in the case of employment and movement, in reality their access is in no way straightforward. Several barriers to accessing these services have been cited by Syrian refugees, including, once again, the language barrier, which produces communication difficulties between refugees and doctors as well as between children and their teachers, and discrimination, which has resulted in refugees being refused access to services. Without access to social services, long-term human capital issues persist and, in turn, access to skilled labour opportunities becomes yet more problematic.

From the above discussion, it has become clear that for Syrian refugees to capitalise on their legal freedoms in Turkey and thus establish a real expansion of individual freedom, reform is necessary at both the national and international levels. For instance, job training is required for local host communities who have become unemployed, as well as for refugees to ensure that their qualifications can be transferred to the Turkish labour market. Improved education access is also paramount for refugees, including language classes for children and adults. The Turkish government must also make an active effort to prevent the formation of illicit markets and minimum wage violations, which are negatively impacting refugees and members of host communities alike. However, such reforms will not be cheap, and it should not be the Turkish government's responsibility to both provide physical refuge and fully support the financial requirements associated with hosting alone: the international community must do better.

Overall, it has been shown that communal solidarity and individual freedom create a perfect allyship which ensures that, in the case of a refugee crisis, both the refugees and their local host communities can create mutually beneficial relationships, illustrated through the examples of the Bidibidi and Buduburam refugee settlements. However, in many cases (as in Turkey), legal freedoms afforded to refugees do not materialise into a true expansion of their individual freedom. Without true individual freedom, host communities become far less interested in creating communal solidarity, and the most marginalised members of society are the most likely to lose out. Furthermore, as refugees become more dependent upon aid, they are less able to benefit one another through the creation of employment opportunities or the sharing of resources. Hence, it is vital that in both policy and scholarly circles we move beyond surface-level understandings of what is meant by individual freedom to gain a genuine appreciation for the mutually advantageous relationship that it has with communal solidarity.

# Nick Inman

*Special Mention*

Do you mind if I insult you? I mean: do I have the right to call you names, sneer at you, make scathing remarks about you if I so wish? It is a free country, isn't it? We have free speech. We must be able to exchange opinions and feelings. Or should I curb my impulse, censor myself out of respect for your feelings? You wouldn't make me do that, would you? It seems to me that we have to balance your interests, my freedom, and the good of society. There is something that needs thinking through here.

If I lived in the woods of Michigan – far from neighbours, off-grid, without technology, and expecting nothing from anyone – the question would be meaningless. There, I could do what I wanted, within the limits set by nature. There would be no one to be rude to. No one who could take offence. 'Anti-social' would have no meaning. I would be truly free.

But my life is not like that. I live and move within

human groups. My absolute freedom is inevitably compromised.

I am part of several groups. I am born into a family that is defined by its invisible blood ties and web of relationships. I live in a village that is geographical as well as political, and this village is part of a country that imposes laws on me and expects me to pay taxes. Other groups I may choose for myself: a professional organisation, a religion, a sports club, and so on. These collectivities overlap and I overlap them; I live at least half in all of them.

All groups function in much the same way, whatever their size or nature. They all have four aspects to them.

To begin with, they are all fictitious, abstract human contrivances. You can't weigh or measure a collective noun. You can't see the blood or the relationships that tie a family together. The geography of North America exists, but you cannot see the United States from space. We believe in groups for our own convenience.

Secondly, a group is a paradox. It is a singular made from a plural. It is both its members individually and a whole. The English language honours this ambiguity by allowing us to say 'the committee is' or 'the committee are' depending on the sense of the statement.

Thirdly, most groups try to become 'real', and to endure, by creating structures. An anarchist may say that groups can exist without structure, but the evidence suggests otherwise. Loose collectives may find ways to function for a time, but outside forces always spoil the party. Witness Paris in 1871 and Barcelona in 1939.

There are two means by which a group makes itself real. For one thing, it invents practical structures and appoints personnel. At the very least, a club must have a management committee, a treasurer, and a list of members. Advanced groups conceal their abstract nature – literally set themselves in stone – by building presidential palaces and parliaments.

As important as the practical arrangements is ideology. A group has to make insiders and outsiders believe in it. It has to convince members that they are connected and have interests in common, that solidarity is necessary. Ideology is promoted through symbols such as flags, ethics such as patriotism, taboos, and the endless repetition of the words 'we/us' and 'they/them'.

Fourthly, every group must settle on a trade-off between cohesion (group ethos) and the individual freedom of its members.

There are two extremes on the cohesion-versus-freedom continuum.

Some groups try to regulate all envisagable freedoms, and members are thus only able to do what is not prohibited by the rules. Medieval feudal society, for example, governed by religion and a God-appointed aristocracy, worked like this. This approach produces stability and predictability, or stuckness if you prefer. The future is written by tradition. Such a society is unable to develop, and its leaders do not want it to. However, rigidity can provoke all manner of ills: an uncontrollable black market, hypocrisy, and secret bad behaviour. Ultimately, it can result in violent protest or revolution.

Individual freedom encourages and rewards initiative and innovation, but if there is 'too much' freedom, there is nothing to bind members together. There is nothing to talk about at the dinner table, and it can be impossible to make plans. Everything becomes vague and relative. Selfishness becomes a virtue, leading to the disintegration of the group in separatism.

As individuals, we learn to figure out what kinds of groups we belong to and how free they let us be. In early childhood, our freedom is limited by the adults in charge of us – parents, guardians, teachers – and by what the people around us think (good behaviour is smiled upon; bad behaviour produces a frown; if you want sweets, you know what to do). Then, as we grow older, we become aware of a more serious curb to the freedom we like to think we have. The government, or rather the state, lays down laws, and there are serious penalties for believing that they do not apply to us.

And so we come to the modern concept of freedom.

Until the Enlightenment and the American and French revolutions, no one spoke of freedom in the way that we do. Prior to those upheavals, freedom was in the gift of God or the gods. In the nineteenth century, we definitively handed control over freedom to the nation state. How free you are depends on which country you live in. This principle is theoretically tempered by the notion of universal human rights, but a right is only worth anything if anyone respects it.

The simplest and perhaps most common arrangement in the contemporary world is for the ruler or rulers of the state to decide what freedom its citizens have. He/they enforce his/their own vision of freedom with violence, or more commonly the threat of violence, and various forms of propaganda and intimidation.

In an authoritarian country, you don't get a choice between communal solidarity and individual freedom; the matter is decided for you in favour of service and sacrifice.

There is, however, one kind of state that overtly seeks to optimise the formula, that expects selfless loyalty in return for as much individual freedom as is practicable, and claims to draw its power from the consent of all participants.

Democracy depends on three very simple principles – so simple that many people misunderstand them: free association, egalitarianism, and self-regulation. Citizens theoretically decide their own balance between communal solidarity and individual freedom. It sounds perfect, and the democratic states believe that theirs is the model for all states of the world to copy. It perfectly complements globalised consumer capitalism. In practice, though, democracy is not easy to make work. This is partly because 'freedom' is not such a simple thing.

There is a difference, for example, between notional and actual freedom. I may have the right to free speech but not have free speech in practice. A freedom that is ineffectual is worthless.

There is also a distinction to be drawn between freedom awarded and freedom denied. It could be argued that freedom is not something we need to be given but something which we must stop the state taking away.

There is public freedom and private freedom: why shouldn't I have the right to take any drug I want at home, as long as it doesn't affect you?

And there is freedom with respect to the law. Should I be free to disobey the law if I so choose? Who has the right to judge me or punish me? How do they acquire that right?

Freedom is the bedrock of democracy, and there are no definitive answers. All we can do is face up to the problems and thrash out working solutions between us. The many questions about freedom and collective solidarity that democracy throws up must be openly discussed. Endlessly.

Freedom is not something fixed; it is dynamic and shifting. A democratic society is always moving either towards or away from an ideal balance of freedom versus communal solidarity. We must constantly assess conditions to know in which direction we are heading and to lay out our options for correcting course.

To do that, we have to recognise the obstacles to full, equally shared freedom in a democratic society.

The first of these is privilege. In a democracy, everyone is equal, but in practice people acquire privilege in many ways. They get more than their share of political voice and political influence; they can be said to be more politically free than the rest of us.

The system must have some way to minimalise this distorting effect.

Another warper of freedom is money. The more you have, the more you can buy your freedom. The less you have, the more you are constrained by your circumstances. No one can argue that the poor and hungry are free in anything but a technical sense. Again, a democratic society needs to attend to this, to redistribute, and enable the disadvantaged to attain freedoms that others take for granted.

Privilege and money are both forms of power.

Power, remember, resides equally with citizens. My voice and my vote must be exactly equal to yours, or we do not live in a democracy.

Democracy is government by a free people. It depends for its moral authority on the unambiguous consent of the people. It is this which legitimises the government. The people must be able to freely criticise and sanction the decisions of the government and the actions of the state.

In order for the government to impose demands of communal solidarity, for it to demand that people give up some of their freedoms for the good of all, it must be legitimate. It is easy to create and run a sham democracy, one that talks of freedom but restricts it or allows an uneven distribution.

If the political system succumbs to the corrupting influences of wealth and privilege, it must make adjustments so that it doesn't favour some people and hold back others. It must be forced to make such adjustments, otherwise it is not a democracy and its people will not be free.

At the very least, there must be a constitution, intelligible to all who are affected by it, that lays out the terms and conditions of freedom and communal obligation. This constitution must lay out a mechanism by which everyone has a full and fair choice at elections (not just Party A or Party B because they have the system sewn up between them) and everyone has the same opportunity to reach high office and to hold office holders to account. At the very least, the constitution has to guarantee an electoral system based on proportionality.

The political system must also recognise and honour dissent – a difficult but necessary concept in democracy. Dissent is the only way to confront problems such as a politician claiming to be acting in the interests of freedom when they are doing the opposite. For instance, if the country goes to war without a democratic mandate and with no way to hold decision makers accountable, the people cannot be free. Young people sent to fight will be deprived of their freedom (even the ultimate freedom, to go on living) without a clear objective of the common good. In such circumstances, communal solidarity is usually known as 'patriotism'.

Dissent, of course, cannot be orchestrated by the system itself. It is up to us. You and I need to preserve each other's freedom. But we must take care. I may have the free right to insult you, but I can choose how I exercise that right. I must take into account the conditions prevailing and anyone affected by my use of my freedom: you, other people, the society we are part of. I need a virtue to guide me. 'Communal solidarity' is somewhat vague and impersonal. Far better is 'responsibility'.

The internet has rendered responsibility old fashioned.

Our contemporary culture is built on the simplification of the maxim of Aleister Crowley: 'Do what thou wilt'. We need to rediscover the meaning of responsibility and promote understanding of it.

Responsibility is the interface between what I want and what I have to do for the good of whichever group I am involved in, from my family to my nation state. It is a way of moderating my desires without denying myself in a repressive way.

It governs the grey, fluid, dynamic area between right and duty. It is how I behave even if no one is looking.

It is independent of money, power, good looks, privilege, and skills. It doesn't require orders and it cannot be managed by anyone except me. It cannot be legislated for, but it can be nurtured by encouragement. How much better politics would be if we rewarded responsibility instead of rhetoric, if the media undertook its role with greater diligence and less concern for clicks.

To be responsible is to make the effort to be aware and to think; it is to take ownership of my words and my actions; it is to make reasoned moral decisions that I can defend if I have to. It generates 'healthy' guilt and shame; it recognises the need for apologising or correcting my mistakes.

It is how you and I will work things out between us, whether or not there are laws or rules. Life is a series of specific situations, and there are no general principles that will fit all circumstances.

If you and I are both responsible – or at least we strive to be so – we may not even need to ask the question I began with. If we can have a reasoned discussion about the conflict between communal solidarity and individual freedom, I doubt that either of us will feel the need to be gratuitously rude. I retain the right, of course, to insult you if I believe it is the right thing to do, but I am also ready to be held responsible for my words and the tone of my voice.

# Beninio McDonough-Tranza

*Special Mention*

In August 1980 Anna Walentynowicz, a crane operator at the Lenin Shipyard in Gdansk, was sacked after thirty years of work and only five months before she was due to retire. The autocratic management of the shipyard had chosen to punish her for working to build a free trade union, a serious offence in a self-declared workers' state. However, far from disciplining its workforce, the management unwittingly triggered an occupation of the shipyards and a mass strike which would, in a matter of weeks, spread across the nation. The slogan of the shipyard workers, 'there is no freedom without solidarity', soon reverberated across the nation as millions of other workers, seeing their own oppression and their hopes reflected in the struggle of the shipyards, risked their livelihoods and security to join the strike. In only one month, the Communist government was forced to concede defeat and recognise the first free trade union in the Eastern Bloc. In recognition of the fundamental ideals of the shipyard strike, and of the source of its strength, the new union christened itself Solidarność ('Solidarity').

Today the Solidarity movement is widely venerated, particularly in Europe, where it is regarded as a formative moment in the creation of the EU and an embodiment of what Hans-Gert Pöttering has termed the European 'community of values'. As I write this essay, countries across the world are in the process of commemorating its forty-year anniversary with great fanfare. Today (31 August 2020) I read the speech of the current Polish prime minister Mateusz Morawiecki, who hailed Solidarność as 'a great project that is still unfinished. Those ideals of Solidarity are not only the history of the last forty years. They are also a determinant for the next forty years for the government, society, and our nation.' He was speaking outside the European Solidarity Centre in Gdansk, a gargantuan museum, library, and academic centre established by the EU and the Polish government to act, according to its founding document, as 'a living monument' and 'symbol of the victory of the Solidarity movement's peaceful revolution'. I visited this centre myself for a conference some years ago. Yet to me it appeared as a monument not to the victory of those brave strikers but to the death of their dreams.

The European Solidarity Centre is an architecturally

beautiful structure of cavernous interiors enclosed by high rusted-steel walls, designed to evoke the maritime tradition that built Gdansk and nourished its great strike. But it stands in a desolate wasteland amid abandoned buildings and silent cranes. The shipyards, which once employed more than 20,000 people, have gone through successive bankruptcies since the fall of Communism and today provide work for fewer than 2,000 people. The period of shock therapy, presided over by union leaders-turned-politicians, led to the collapse of Poland's industrial base, spiralling inequality, and the rapid disillusionment of many who had once dreamed of a better life. When Solidarity was legalised, it was the largest trade union in the world, counting on the allegiance of more than 10 million members, but today, like the shipyards in which it was born, it has decayed and has lost almost its entire membership. It is, after all, difficult for any union to organise in an economy where stable skilled work has been increasingly replaced by precarious labour.

Plans have recently been drawn up to 'revitalise' Gdansk by converting the abandoned shipyard buildings into a 'young city' of luxury apartments, shops, and cafés catering to the tourist trade. What more poignant comment could there be on the failure of solidarity? When the Gdansk strikers began their struggle, they nailed twenty-one demands to the shipyard gates, which still stand today as a monument to the movement. If one of their grandchildren today gazed up at those demands on her way to work in one of the new cafés of the 'young city', she would find them hopelessly utopian. A reduction of the retirement age to fifty, guaranteed wage increases in line with inflation, guaranteed housing, three years' paid maternity leave – how could they have dreamed such things were possible? It's true that the most famous demand, for free trade unions, has of course been achieved, but if our young Polish worker – inspired perhaps by the demands of her grandparents – tried to organise her colleagues, she would be fired from the café as surely as Anna Walentynowicz was sacked from the shipyard. Perhaps it would be better if she made use of the new freedoms granted by European citizenship to sell coffee in Berlin or Dublin for slightly higher wages instead.

The path followed by Poland is far from unique. It is merely an extreme example of trends which are mirrored across modern Europe. There are few international organisations that employ the language of solidarity as much as the European Union. The EU Charter of Fundamental Rights even includes a set of 'solidarity rights' such as the rights to healthcare, environmental protection, protection in the event of unfair dismissal, and social security. However, the actual attainment of these rights is more difficult today than when the charter was signed in virtually every EU country. While individual rights have, in many respects, been enhanced in law, social protections are increasingly under threat. The institutions that have historically helped foster communal solidarity, such as trade unions, have decayed across the continent, and working conditions are, as a result, worsening every year. As the economist Guy Standing has warned, the insecurity of labour and social income has led to the increasing prominence of a 'precariat', stuck 'in career-less jobs, without traditions of social memory' who find 'the probability of upward social mobility or of gaining a "decent" income … permanently reduced.'

As the social ties that used to bind society together have weakened, a new vision of community based on racial exclusivity and resentment has developed, promoted by far-right demagogues who flourish in a world of unchecked individualism. They have sought to foster an ersatz solidarity based, increasingly, on hostility to migrants and refugees. Marine Le Pen, for instance, has argued that solidarity must be established 'among French citizens' and is threatened by the development of a multicultural community. Here, again, Poland serves as a worrying portent for the future. Morawiecki, who speaks today of the virtues of solidarity, leads one of the most reactionary governments in Europe. The popularity of his ruling Law and Justice Party is a direct consequence of the collapse of Solidarność and has been nurtured by increasing disillusionment under which rabidly nationalist visions of community flourish.

Does this suggest that today we have sacrificed social solidarity for greater personal freedom? This is certainly the opinion of many liberal political thinkers who, building on the legacy of John Stuart Mill, tend to conceptualise solidarity as the inverse of individual liberty. Anthony Giddens has, according to Charles Heying, argued that the Enlightenment 'unlocked our capacity to create worlds of our own choosing' but left us cast 'adrift' in a society bereft of 'the certainties of place, tradition, and communal solidarity.' Progressives like Giddens regard this development with trepidation and seek to defend institutions of social welfare and redistributive taxation. On the other hand, Libertarians like Robert Nozick exalt the same processes, arguing that the demands of institutionalised social solidarity threaten individual liberty and that the state should be further eroded.

Yet what all these thinkers share, despite their many differences, is the presumption that society is built on a balance between individual freedom and communal solidarity. The basic approach is encapsulated succinctly in an influential 1948 lecture by Bertrand Russell in which he proposed to consider the 'fundamental problem' of how 'we combine that degree of individual initiative which is necessary for progress with the degree of social cohesion that is necessary for survival'. Though Nozick and Giddens would disagree on their answer, both would, I think, agree that Russell's question is well framed. Giddens thinks that the balance has shifted too much in favour of individual liberty, while Nozick argues that it has not gone far enough, but both conceptualise solidarity and personal freedom as opposing values. The task of political theory is, as it were, to ascertain in what proportions they should be combined to sustain a liberal democracy.

Yet, as the strikers at Gdansk realised, the very question relies on a false dichotomy. Their rallying cry, 'there is no freedom without solidarity', was not just a good slogan but a basic fact of life. In what sense does our society grant anyone except the relatively privileged the ability to 'create worlds of our own choosing'? Does the modern precariat trapped in an endless cycle of low-paid and demeaning temporary work have the luxury of what liberal theorists like to call 'self-authorship'? We live in a world in which freedom is, as one nineteenth-century jurist acidly commented, like the Ritz hotel: everyone is free to go in, but only a certain few can afford it. I am relatively free because I am relatively privileged. I live in a nice house in London. I have the opportunity to write essays on political theory and travel to EU-funded conferences in Poland. To suggest that my freedom is equivalent to, for example, the cleaners who work in the conference centre would be ridiculous. We are all, of course, subject to the same rule of law, a law which, as the French writer and thinker Anatole France once said, in its majestic equality 'forbids the rich as well as the poor to sleep under bridges, to beg in the streets, and to steal bread', but in no meaningful sense do we have equal levels of freedom.

Real freedom, as opposed to abstract rights, is not a value opposed to the institutions of communal solidarity but, in fact, depends on the expansion of social ties. It is only by increasing the power of society that we may ever hope to achieve genuine liberty. This is masked by the dominance of what the political scientist C. B. Macpherson has aptly termed 'the political theory of possessive individualism', an ideology that sees freedom as the absence of social obligation. However, it has been strikingly illustrated by the current pandemic, which has all too clearly demonstrated the dependence of each person on the social whole. The pandemic has also tragically illustrated the extent to which social inequality undermines personal liberty. Everyone agrees that health is necessary to freedom, yet we are today living through a crisis in which the poor are, quite literally, being forced to risk their lives for the survival of the rich. In the UK, where I live, the 'essential workers' who have kept society functioning during this crisis, such as cleaners, super-market cashiers, delivery drivers, fruit pickers, nurses, bus drivers, and countless others, have been forced to go into work, often for very low pay and at great personal risk, while those of us who are more privileged isolate at home. These workers are disproportionately poorer, more vulnerable, and from ethnic minority backgrounds – unsurprisingly, they have also had a disproportionately higher rate of death than the more comfortable classes who have relied on their labour.

Others have, of course, been even less lucky. When I travelled home from Euston station earlier this week, I passed three homeless men wrapped in sleeping bags and begging. At the beginning of the first UK lockdown (in March 2020), the state guaranteed accommodation for homeless people and requisitioned hotel rooms to provide it, housing 1,400 people in London alone. This, of course, greatly increased the 'freedom' and personal autonomy of homeless people – it is hard to consider yourself the author of your own destiny when you sleep on the streets – but it was considered a rather unfortunate imposition on the rest of us who paid the bill through taxation. In May 2020, at a peak of the pandemic, the funding for the scheme was quietly ended, and homeless people are now back on the streets (although local government in London has kindly assured them that funding will be made available so that shelters are able to implement social distancing). Is there any better illustration of how little individual freedom means in a society riven by inequality?

Individual freedom cannot be discussed in the abstract, for the liberty of the poor and disadvantaged can only be attained by changing the conditions of their oppression and this means, in practice, redistributing wealth and power. Put simply, the 'individual freedom' of the vast majority of people can only be attained by reducing the 'individual freedom' of the privileged. There is thus no opposition between freedom and social obligation – but there is an opposition between the freedoms of the rich and the poor, the oppressed and the oppressor, the hungry and the fed.

Moreover, every extension of individual rights is, at the same time, a limitation of the rights of other individuals. For instance, I have the freedom to stay in any hotel I choose (provided I can afford it), but this implies that the hotel owners do not have the right to refuse me. My freedom is premised on the curtailment of their freedom. If society valued our respective positions differently, it could well change the situation. Indeed, this particular right was fairly recently established in UK law when a gay couple won their case against a hotel that refused them a room.

Many other examples could be elicited. In the UK, there are 300,000 Gypsies and Travellers, who are one of the most ostracised ethnic minority groups in the country. From 2005, there was an increasingly vicious xenophobic campaign in the national press, detailed in Imogen Tyler's *Revolting Subjects*, which culminated in legal changes granting local government much greater leeway to evict them from occupied land and gave residents the right to sit on councils that could deny planning permission to Traveller camps. Needless to say, this extension of rights to residents severely curtailed the freedom of Travellers.

These examples illustrate that what we see as a limitation of our freedom, and how much freedom we seek to give to others, depends on the extent to which we see one another as human beings. No hotel owner who wasn't homophobic would consider their inability to reject guests based on sexual preference an infringement of their rights. If Gypsies and Travellers were regarded as full human beings in Britain, their social presence would not be considered an affront to, and an infringement of, the freedom of the majority population. If we recognised the common humanity of homeless people, we would agree with Martin Luther King Jr. that true compassion cannot mean merely 'flinging a coin to a beggar' but comes when we see that 'an edifice which produces beggars needs restructuring'. This illustrates the centrality of solidarity to any discussion of freedom. For what 'solidarity' means, in essence, is the recognition of common humanity in the Other and a commitment to struggle with them.

The word 'solidarity' has an interesting, if little known, history. It was first coined as a political concept by the utopian socialist Pierre Leroux, who defined it in his great work *De l'humanité* as a commitment to humanity, a recognition that the individual exists as part of society and finds fulfilment only through the development of social bonds by which egoism can be overcome. This has often been forgotten because there is another understanding of the term, derived from the philosopher Auguste Comte and formulated most cogently by the sociologist Émile Durkheim, which defines solidarity in a purely functional sense as those ties which bind a society together. For Durkheim solidarity is social glue designed to reduce tensions, but for Leroux solidarity is an active emotion designed to transform and ultimately transcend our society. Durkheim, for instance, argues that migration undermines solidarity by breaking existing social bonds, whereas for Leroux true solidarity can only be achieved as national and parochial identities are superseded. Solidarity in this sense is not the medicine for tension but is, in fact, achieved through common struggle. It is a concept analogous to the traditional Christian ideal of love.

When we act in solidarity, we do not see sacrifices as limitations of our freedom but as expressions of our humanity. In a profound sense, indeed, it is by developing solidarity that we express and develop our own freedom. We live in an atomised society in which individuals are encouraged to jealously protect their own alienation. This rampant individualism leads not only to the material degradation of the poor and disadvantaged but also to the moral degradation of the privileged. As Leroux wrote,

> If forgetting that you are united to humanity, you make yourself an egoist, you would have the solitary pleasures of a single man, that is to say of a man horribly incomplete and who lacks the necessary milieu for his true existence; you would be an imperfect being, a sort of monster.

John Stuart Mill, the great prophet of individual liberty, once asked, 'What more or better can be said of any condition of human affairs, than that it brings human beings themselves nearer to the best thing they can be?' This is a fine sentiment, but if our own society is judged against it, we must be found sorely lacking. Allowing an individual to develop as 'the best thing they can be' requires that we see our own humanity embodied in others, that we strive to build a world in which each person, not only a privileged few, can develop their capacities and give voice to their hopes, and that we define success not based on our own freedom of action but on the freedom of the weakest and most disadvantaged among us. When the Gdansk strike began, Anna Walentynowicz said that our aim must not be 'to secure a somewhat thicker slice of bread today, even if this would make us happy ... Our main duty is to consider the needs of others ... Our day-to-day motto should be: "Your problems are also my problems". I hope that when we come to celebrate the eighty-year anniversary of Solidarność, our world will have moved somewhat closer to her ideal than it has so far.

# Acknowledgements

I should like to thank this year's judges of the Hubert Butler Essay Prize – Catriona Crowe, Roy Foster (chair), Nicholas Grene, Eva Hoffman, and Barbara Schwepcke – who all gave their time, expertise, and help with characteristic generosity and good humour. The prize would not have been possible without Olga Barry and her superb team at the Kilkenny Arts Festival, who gave their invaluable support and excellent promotion of the prize. Hubert Butler's family – especially his daughter and son-in-law, Julia and Dick Crampton, and their daughter Cordelia Gelly and her husband James – has been fantastically helpful throughout. Thanks also go to Ambassador Adrian O'Neill and his colleagues at the Embassy of Ireland in London; Adrian Arena of the Oak Foundation; David Gelber at *Literary Review*; Eugene Downes at the Irish Department of Foreign Affairs; Harry Hall and Jo Stimfield at Haus Publishing; our Honorary Patron, John Banville; and, last but very much not least, to Ireland's President Michael D. Higgins for his generous and thoughtful words that introduce this year's winning essays.

– Jeremy O'Sullivan, *Hubert Butler Essay Prize*

# The Hubert Butler Essay Prize

The annual Hubert Butler Essay Prize was founded by Jeremy O'Sullivan in 2018 to honour Hubert Butler, to promote his work, and to encourage the art of essay writing. As of 2022, O'Sullivan will run the prize on behalf of the Kilkenny Arts Festival. The 2020 prize was supported by Kilkenny Arts Festival to mark the 120th anniversary of Butler's birth.

The prize reflects Butler's interest in the common ground between the European nation states that emerged after the First World War; his concern with the position of religious and ethnic minorities; his life and writings as an encapsulation of the mantra 'Think globally, act locally'; the importance of the individual conscience; and his work with refugees.

Hubert Butler was born in Kilkenny in 1900, and he travelled extensively throughout Europe during his life. With his wife, Peggy, he founded the Kilkenny Lectures to encourage dialogue between the people of Northern Ireland and the Republic, and he found international recognition in his eighties for his essay collections *Escape from the Anthill*, *The Children of Drancy*, and *Grandmother and Wolfe Tone*. He died in 1991.

## HAUS CURIOSITIES

Inspired by the topical pamphlets of the interwar years, as well as by Einstein's advice to 'never lose a holy curiosity', the series presents short works of opinion and analysis by notable figures. Under the guidance of the series editor, Peter Hennessy, Haus Curiosities have been published since 2014.

Welcoming contributions from a diverse pool of authors, the series aims to reinstate the concise and incisive booklet as a powerful strand of politico-literary life, amplifying the voices of those who have something urgent to say about a topical theme.